ROANOKE COLONY

This series features unsolved mysteries, urban legends, and other curious stories. Each creepy, shocking, or befuddling book focuses on what people believe and hear. True or not? That's for you to decide!

45th Parallel Press

Published in the United States of America by Cherry Lake Publishing
Ann Arbor, Michigan
www.cherrylakepublishing.com

Reading Adviser: Marla Conn MS, Ed., Literacy specialist, Read-Ability, Inc.
Book Designer: Felicia Macheske

Photo Credits: © andreiuc88/Shutterstock.com, cover; © Ahturner/Shutterstock.com, 5; © KobchaiMa/
Shutterstock.com, 7; © New York Public Library Digital Collections, 8; © Joseph Sohm/Shutterstock.com, 11;
© Ryszard Filipowicz/Shutterstock.com, 13; © Georgios Kollidas/Shutterstock.com, 15; © KI Petro/Shutterstock.
com, 16; © Pi-Lens/Shutterstock.com, 18; © Wallenrock/Shutterstock.com, 21; © Sergey Shubin/Shutterstock.com,
22; © jctabb/Shutterstock.com, 25; © FutroZen/Shutterstock.com, 26; © Dario Lo Presti/Shutterstock.com, 29

Graphic Elements Throughout: © iofoto/Shutterstock.com; © COLCU/Shutterstock.com; © spacedrone808/
Shutterstock.com; © rf.vector.stock/Shutterstock.com; © donatas1205/Shutterstock.com; © cluckva/
Shutterstock.com; © Eky Studio/Shutterstock.com

45th Parallel Press is an imprint of Cherry Lake Publishing.

Library of Congress Cataloging-in-Publication Data has been filed and is available at catalog.loc.gov

Cherry Lake Publishing would like to acknowledge the work of The Partnership for 21st Century Skills.
Please visit *www.p21.org* for more information.

Printed in the United States of America
Corporate Graphics

TABLE OF CONTENTS

Chapter One

DARE TO BE BORN

Who was Virginia Dare? What is the "white doe" story? What are the Dare Stones?

Virginia Dare was born on August 18, 1587. She was born in America. She was the first English baby born in America. People say she was the first Christian born in America.

Dare's parents were Ananias and Eleanor. They traveled from England. They landed on Roanoke Island. This area was part of the Virginia **Colony**. Colony means an area controlled by another country. Virginia was named after the Virgin Queen. The Virgin

Queen was Queen Elizabeth. She ruled England.

Dare disappeared. There are many stories about Dare. Some people think she was killed. Some think she married a Native American chief.

The American colonies were a dangerous place for children.

CONSIDER THE EVIDENCE

"La Virginea Pars" map is a special map. It's a map of Roanoke Island. Governor John White made it. He did this in 1585. Historians saw two patches. The patches are made of the same paper as the map. They covered something up. Historians studied the patches. They put it against a special light. They found hidden markings. They found a tiny star. It has four points. It has a blue outline. It's red. This might be where the colonists went. Some experts think it represents a fort. Others think it's a secret location. They think White covered it up. White wanted to avoid spies.

Some people think she turned into a white **doe**. A doe is a female deer. Dare was beautiful. A man wanted to marry her. So did a **sorcerer**. A sorcerer is a male witch. Dare rejected him. The sorcerer got mad. He turned Dare into a white doe. The man wanted to save her. He made a magical arrow. This would make Dare human again. He found the white doe. He shot. The white doe turned into Dare. But another man shot an arrow, too. He killed Dare. Today, people report seeing a white doe on Roanoke Island. They think it's Dare's ghost.

The white doe roams Roanoke Island.

The Virginia Colony was one of the original thirteen colonies.

The "Dare Stones" were found in the 1930s. They were found in states close to Roanoke Island. There are over 40 stones. Messages are carved into them. Dare's mother is believed to have written them.

A **tourist** found the first stone. Tourists are visitors. He took it to a university. Experts studied it. One side said Ananias and Virginia were dead. The other side said Native Americans attacked them. It was signed "EWD." These are Eleanor Dare's initials.

Experts aren't sure if the stones are real. Some experts think they're fake. Some think only the first stone is real.

Chapter Two

BUILDING A WHOLE NEW WORLD

Where is Roanoke Island? What was the point of Dare's colony?

Roanoke Island is about 8 miles (13 kilometers) long. It's about 2 miles (3 km) wide. It's in North Carolina. It's in Dare County. It's in the Outer Banks. It has many storms. It has many shipwrecks.

Virginia Dare's group lived on Roanoke. They built houses together. Then, they all disappeared. No one really knows what happened. They're known as the Lost Colony. There were about 90 men. There were about 20 women. There were about 10 children.

They were supposed to settle in the "New World."
That's what the English called the Americas. The
English wanted more land. Roanoke was the first
English settlement.

Roanoke Island is named after Native Americans who had lived there.

SPOTLIGHT
BIOGRAPHY

Chief Manteo was a Croatoan. He lived on Roanoke Island. In 1585, the English went to Roanoke. They arrived too late to plant crops. They didn't have food. Manteo helped them. He fed them. The English liked him. They took him to England twice. He traveled with Governor John White back to Roanoke. In 1587, Manteo was baptized. He became a member of the Church of England. He was the first Native American to do so. Manteo was a friend to the settlers. He taught them things. He guided them. He translated for them. Historians aren't sure what happened to him. Some think he may have left with the Roanoke colonists.

There were other Roanoke colonists. The first group came in 1584. They explored. They mapped the land. They fought with Native Americans. They built a fort. But they missed England. They went back.

Dare's group came in 1587. They were supposed to build **permanent** homes. Permanent means forever. Dare's group was the first to include **civilians**. Civilians means people who aren't in the military. They included women and children.

Roanoke was colonized before other settlements. It happened 22 years before Jamestown. It happened 37 years before Plymouth.

The English wanted to expand their empire.

Chapter Three

MYSTERIOUSLY MISSING

Who was Sir Walter Raleigh? Who was John White? What did White find in Roanoke?

Sir Walter Raleigh was an explorer. He wanted to colonize America. He got permission from Queen Elizabeth. He colonized what is now the state of Virginia. This happened in 1584. Raleigh wanted more land. He put John White in charge. He sent White to Chesapeake Bay. White was Virginia Dare's grandfather. White left England. He took his family with him.

The colonists stopped in Roanoke. They checked for survivors. They found a skeleton. Simon Fernandez was the ship's captain. He didn't want to go to Chesapeake Bay. He made the colonists stay in Roanoke. He left them there. The colonists settled there instead.

Sir Walter Raleigh funded the trips.

The settlement was abandoned.

White became governor. Soon, Virginia Dare was born. The colonists fought with Native Americans. Some colonists died. They ran out of supplies. They wanted White to go back to England. They wanted him to bring back supplies. White returned to England. He didn't get much help. He had a hard time getting back. England was fighting Spain. White was stuck. He couldn't leave for 3 years.

White returned to Roanoke on August 18, 1590. This was Dare's third birthday. White came back to nothing. People were gone. Houses were taken down. There were no signs of struggle. There was only a fence.

Today, Croatoan is called Hatteras Island.

White found two clues. "Croatoan" was carved into a fence post. "Cro" was carved into a tree. Croatoan was the name of a nearby island. It was also the name of a friendly Native American tribe.

White had talked to the colonists before he left. He came up with a plan. He told them to carve a special cross. This meant they were forced to leave. He didn't see a cross. So, he thought the colonists were fine. He didn't see dead bodies. He didn't see bones.

He wanted to search Croatoan Island. But there was a bad storm. He had to return to England. He never heard from the colonists again.

REAL-WORLD
CONNECTION

Pripyat is a city. It's in northern Ukraine. It used to be an exciting town. It used to have 50,000 people. But something bad happened. The Chernobyl nuclear power plant exploded. It was the worst man-made nuclear disaster. Fire burned for 9 days. Radiation was released into the air. Radiation is bad energy. It's poisonous. Many people died. This destroyed Pripyat. People left for safety. The city turned into a ghost town. It's been abandoned for over 30 years. Buildings are run down. Trash is on the ground. Plants have taken over building walls. Radioactive wolves live in the woods. Scientists think Pripyat will be unsafe for at least 24,000 years.

Chapter Four

THERE'S ALWAYS ALIENS!

Why is Roanoke Colony such a mystery? Who is Sir Francis Walsingham? What are other explanations for Roanoke Colony?

The people were lost. The place was lost, as well. No one knows exactly where it is. The colonists didn't keep good records. There were no **remnants**. Remnants are leftover things. It's a mystery. So, people made up stories. They tried to explain what happened.

Some think it's a story of **betrayal**. Betrayal is when people are disloyal. Sir Francis Walsingham worked for Queen Elizabeth. He was her "spymaster." He was jealous of Raleigh. He wanted the Roanoke

Colony to fail. He had saved Simon Fernandez's life. So, Fernandez owed him a favor. Walsingham had Fernandez take the colonists to Roanoke. He also delayed White in England.

Some historians think the site of the colony is now underwater.

How could over 100 people disappear? They left in a short time. They left no trace. There were no bodies. That confused people.

Some people think **aliens** are to blame. Aliens are beings from outer space. They kidnapped the colonists. They beamed them up. They took their bodies away. They forced the colonists to live on a faraway planet. They studied them.

Other people think the colonists ate each other. This is called **cannibalism**. The colonists lived apart from others. They were hungry. They ran out of food. So, they fed on each other.

Some people blame zombies.

INVESTIGATION
TIPS

- Use tools to help find buried objects. Use a metal detector. It finds buried metal. Use a magnetometer. It finds iron and magnetic material. Use a GPR. GPR is ground-penetrating radar. It sends radio waves into the ground. Waves bounce off things buried underground.

- Make a map. Use a lidar. It's a light radar. It uses light instead of radio waves. It shows things that can't be seen.

- Know where to look. Use a GPS. GPS stands for global positioning system. It helps you find locations.

- There are lots of storms in the Outer Banks. Learn about hurricane safety.

- Study early U.S. history.

Chapter Five

HIDING IN PLAIN SIGHT

How do experts explain the Roanoke Colony? What happened with the Native Americans? What is the Lumbee Connection?

Experts have different ideas. They studied the area. They studied sources. They studied history. Some think the colonists died from sickness. Many early settlers died that way. But where are the bodies?

The English and Spanish were at war. Both tried to get land in the New World. Spanish settlers lived in Florida. Some people think they killed the colonists. But the Spanish didn't find the area until 1600.

Some Native Americans didn't like the English. They could've killed the males. They got rid of the bodies. They captured women and children. They made them into slaves. They traded them to other tribes.

Some think there was a bad storm.

There were many Native American tribes in the area.

Most experts think the colonists moved in with Native Americans. They split up. They formed small groups. They moved in with different tribes. No one tribe could take in all the colonists. Some moved in with the Croatoans. Some moved in with the Chowanoke.

There was a report. It was written in 1612. It described English houses. The houses had two floors. They had stone walls. Experts think colonists taught Native Americans how to build these houses. Reports also stated there were white people in the tribes. People saw "gray-eyed" Native Americans. They saw Native Americans with blonde hair.

EXPLAINED BY SCIENCE

Scientists studied old trees around Roanoke Island. They studied tree rings. Tree rings are growth rings. They tell how old trees are. They tell about the environment. Scientists determined that the Roanoke colonists arrived at a bad time. There was a major drought in North Carolina. Droughts are dry spells. It was the worst drought in 800 years. This happened from 1587 to 1589. The tree rings were narrow and thin. This means the Roanoke colonists had no fresh water. They didn't have water to drink. They didn't have water for their crops. It makes sense that the colonists moved. They needed to find fresh water.

Native American groups mixed. People from different groups married. They had children. This created a new group. One of these groups is the Lumbee tribe.

Lumbees live in North Carolina. They're linked to the Roanoke colonists. This is called the Lumbee Connection. Some had the same last names. Some were able to read and write English. Some had light eyes. Some had light hair color. Some were Christians.

If this is true, then Roanoke colonists aren't lost. They became a new group. But what really happened? It doesn't matter. The Roanoke Colony lives in people's imaginations.

· Not everyone believes in the Lumbee Connection.

DID YOU KNOW?

- Virginia Dare was on a U.S. coin in 1937. The coin was a half-dollar. This was the first time a child was on U.S. money.

- A bridge was built to Roanoke Island. The bridge is called the Virginia Dare Memorial Bridge. It's 5.2 miles (8.4 km) long. It's the longest bridge in North Carolina.

- Some people think Roanoke colonists tried to sail back to England. They think the colonists got lost at sea. But this idea doesn't make sense. The colonists wanted to build a new colony. So, why would they leave? Plus, they didn't have enough supplies. They weren't prepared to make the trip.

- *The Lost Colony* is an outdoor play. It has songs. It has dances. It's performed in Manteo. It shows the events leading to the colonists' disappearance.

- *American Horror Story* is a popular TV show. Its sixth season is based on the Roanoke Colony.

- The Wright brothers' first flight took place on the Outer Banks on December 17, 1903.

- Jamestown Colony was established in 1607. Some of those colonists searched for the Roanoke Colony.

CONSIDER THIS!

Take a Position: Reread Chapters Four and Five. What do you think happened to the Lost Colony? Which theory makes sense to you? Argue your point with reasons and evidence.

Say What? Explain who Virginia Dare is. Explain why she's important to U.S. history. Explain how she's connected to the Lost Colony.

Think About It! Research other "lost" cities. Examples are the City of the Monkey God and Machu Picchu. What does it mean to be "lost"? How are these cities different from the Roanoke Colony? How are they the same?

LEARN MORE

- Blake, Kevin. *Roanoke Island: The Town That Vanished*. New York: Bearport Publishing, 2015.

- Levy, Janey. *Roanoke: The Lost Colony*. New York: Gareth Stevens Publishing, 2015.

- McAneney, Caitlin. *The Lost Colony of Roanoke*. New York: PowerKids Press, 2016.

GLOSSARY

aliens (AY-lee-uhnz) beings from outer space

betrayal (bih-TRAY-uhl) when people are disloyal

cannibalism (KAN-uh-buhl-ih-zim) species eating members of their own species

civilians (suh-VIL-yuhnz) nonmilitary citizens

colony (KAH-luh-nee) group, area controlled by another country

doe (DOH) female deer

permanent (PUR-muh-nuhnt) forever

remnants (REM-nuhnts) leftovers, things remaining

sorcerer (SOR-sur-er) male witch

tourist (TOOR-ist) visitor

INDEX

ABOUT THE AUTHOR

Dr. Virginia Loh-Hagan is an author, university professor, former classroom teacher, and curriculum designer. She has vacationed in the Outer Banks many times. She lives in San Diego with her very tall husband and very naughty dogs. To learn more about her, visit www.virginialoh.com.